Network Mailer 6

NETWORK MAILERS
GIFT GIVING FINANCIAL
INVITATION AND PROSPECT

EARN $2,000,000.00

**LET THIS NETWORK MAILER
SHOW YOU HOW TO DO IT.**

COPYRIGHT 2006, 2015 NETWORK MAILER:

AUTHOR: LARRY SMITH CROCKETT

www.trafford.com
North America & international
toll-free: 1 888 232 4444 (USA & Canada)
fax: 812 355 4082

INTRODUCTION

GIFT GIVING IS AN OUTSTANDING FINANCIAL PROSPECT.

A SIGNIFICANT AMOUNT OF WORKING CASH CAN BE EARNED FOR EVERYONE WORKING THIS.

EVERYONE WORKING THIS FINANCIAL PROSPECT IS COUNTED AS A NETWORK MAILER COMMITTED TO FOLLOWING THE INSTRUCTIONS AS OUTLINED IN THIS BOOKLET.

NETWORK MAILERS REPLYING TO THIS FINANCIAL PROSPECT IS YOUR TOP PRIORITY MAILING LIST.

THIS BUSINESS IS A PROGRESSIVE HOME BASED BUSINESS WITH THE GOAL OF CONTINUING UNTIL YOU HAVE A LARGE VOLUME OF NETWORK MAILERS REPLYING.

WHEN YOU HAVE A GROUP; FOR EXAMPLE, 1,000 NETWORK MAILERS REPLYING TO NETWORK MAILERS YOU WILL HAVE IN YOUR INCOMING MAIL A LARGE VOLUME OF WORKING CASH APPROXIMATELY EVERY TWENTY MAILING DAYS. YOUR OUTGOING GIFTS ARE VERY SMALL COMPARED TO THE INCOMING GIFTS.

KEEP RECORD OF THE REPLYING NETWORK MAILERS MAILING ADDRESSES WITH THE USE OF LARGE PAPER BAGS BECAUSE AS TIME PROGRESSES THEY WILL BE TOO NUMEROUS TO INDEX.

LET YOUR GOAL BE TO CONTINUE UNTIL A GROUP OF NETWORK MAILERS REPLYING TO NETWORK MAILERS IS FORMED.

NETWORK MAILERS REPLYING TO NETWORK MAILERS INCREASES THE RATE OF REPLY AND THE FINANCIAL POTENTIAL.

THIS WORK IS WORTH PATIENT CONTINUANCE.

TO HELP OTHERS, WHERE NEEDED MOST, IS A BETTER MOTIVATION TO WORK THIS FINANCIAL PROSPECT.

FOLLOWING IS A SKETCH OF AN ANALOGICAL MAILING CIRCUIT OR COARSE WHERE NETWORK MAILERS ARE REPLYING TO NETWORK MAILERS:

2°B'S   →C'°3
↑

20 DAYS

TO COMPLETE THE MAILING CIRCUIT

1°A←   D'S°4
                                                     ↓

A FINANCIAL POTENTIAL

FOLLOWING IS A FINANCIAL POTENTIAL WHERE NETWORK MAILERS COMMITTED TO FOLLOWING THE INSTRUCTIONS OUTLINED IN THIS BOOKLET ARE REPLYING TO NETWORK MAILERS WORKING THIS PROSPECT.

A MAILS TO 60 B'S. A IS IN POSITION 3).
AT A 100% RATE, 60 REPLY.

B'S, 60, MAIL 60 EACH TO THE C'S. A IS IN POSITION 2).
THIS IS 3,600 MAILED.
AT A 100% REPLY RATE, 3600 REPLY.

C'S, 3600, MAIL 60 EACH TO THE D'S. A IS IN POSITION 1).
THIS IS 216,000 MAILED.
AT A 100% REPLY RATE, 216000 REPLY.

D'S 216000, MAIL $10 EACH TO A IN POSITION 1).
THIS AMOUNT IS $2,160,000.

THIS FINANCIAL PROSPECT IS WORTH WORKING.

AS YOU CAN SEE FROM THE SKETCH OF THE DIAGRAM OF AN ANALOGICAL MAILING CIRCUIT OR COARSE AND THE FINANCIAL POTENTIAL WHERE NETWORK MAILERS ARE REPLYING TO NETWORK MAILERS, THIS IS A SIGNIFICANT FINANCIAL PROSPECT.

AS TIME IN WORKING THIS BUSINESS PROGRESSES, THE NUMBER OF NETWORK MAILERS REPLYING INCREASES IN VOLUME.

AT RANDOM, REPEAT MAILING TO THESE NETWORK MAILER REPLIERS THE ADVERTISING MAILING CIRCULAR ATTACHED TO THIS BOOKLET (NETWORK MAILERS' MULTITUDE OF GIVERS) ALSO, REPEAT POINT1) AS OFTEN AS YOU RECEIVE THE MAILING CIRCULAR IN YOUR MAIL.

FOR A SOURCE OF REPLY PROSPECTS, WRITE TO THE FOLLOWING COMPANY FOR A FREE COPY OF THEIR ADVERTISING MAGAZINE 'SHORE TO SHORE':

CHA SERVICE
P.O. BOX 1980
ROGUE RIVER, OR 97537

THIS WORK IS NOT MAILING AN ILLEGAL CHAIN LETTER.

AN ILLEGAL CHAIN LETTER IS INVOLVED IN REQUESTING MONEY OR SOMETHING ELSE OF VALUE WITH A PROMISE OF RETURN.

FROM READING POINT 1) OF THE ATTACHED MAILING CIRCULAR, THIS IS A GIFT GIVING FINANCIAL PROSPECT.

IN THIS BUSINESS, NETWORK MAILERS WORK INDEPENDENTLY BUT MAKING THEIR TOP PRIORITY MAILING LIST NETWORK MAILERS COMMITTED TO FOLLOWING THE INSTRUCTIONS AS OUTLINED IN THE ATTACHED MAILING CIRCULAR.

TO SAVE COST IN U.S. MAIL POSTAGE, YOU CAN MAIL THE CIRCULAR TO A MAILING SERVICE COMPANY WHO WILL INCLUDE IT IN THEIR OUT-GOING MAIL.

IT IS THE HUGE MARKET WHICH MAKES THIS FINANCIAL PROSPECT WORK.
FOR EXAMPLE, IT WOULD TAKE 500 YEARS TO MAIL TO 150,000,000 DIFFERENT MAILING ADDRESSES MAILING 300,000 PER YEAR.

NETWORK MAILERS MAILING TO NETWORK MAILERS THE SAME MAILING CIRCULAR AS ATTACHED TO THIS BOOKLET, AS PATIENT CONTINUANCE IS CONTINUED, MAKES THIS GIFT GIVING FINANCIAL PROSPECT WORTH WORKING.

A BETTER MOTIVATION IN WORKING THIS PROSPECT IS TO HELP OTHERS WHERE NEEDED MOST.

THIS PROSPECT WILL WORK FOR YOU IF YOU ARE PROPERLY MOTIVATED.

THE MAIN IDEA IS TO WORK THIS FINANCIAL GIFT GIVING PROSPECT UNTIL YOU HAVE ON RECORD A LARGE VOLUME OF NETWORK MAILERS REPLYING TO NETWORK MAILERS.

SUMMARY

THE ATTACHED CIRCULAR TO THIS BOOKLET IS NOT AN ILLEGAL CHAIN LETTER (NETWORK MAILERS' MULTITUDE OF GIVERS).
FROM POINT 1) OF THIS CIRCULAR YOU CAN CONCLUDE THAT THIS FINANCIAL PROSPECT IS A GIFT GIVING PROSPECT.

AS I STATED PREVIOUSLY, IT TAKES PATIENT CONTINUANCE WITH A BETTER MOTIVATION TO MAKE THIS PROSPECT WORK.

THE MARKET IS VERY HUGE.
500 YEARS TO MAIL TO 150,000,000 DIFFERENT MAILING ADDRESSES MAILING 300,000 PER YEAR MAKES THIS MARKET VERY HUGE.

IT REQUIRES WORKING THIS UNTIL YOU HAVE ON RECORD A LARGE VOLUME OF NETWORK MAILERS REPLYING TO NETWORK MAILERS. IN A GROUP WHERE EVERY NETWORK MAILER HAS THE SAME MAILING LIST OF NETWORK MAILERS, NETWORK MAILERS REPLYING TO NETWORK MAILERS, GREATLY INCREASES THE RATE OF REPLY AND THE FINANCIAL POTENTIAL.

THE NETWORK MAILER'S GIFT BUSINESS: FIRST, COPY THIS MAILING CIRCULAR AS IS FOR YOUR RECORD. THIS IS AN INVITATION TO A SIGNIFICANT FINANCIAL PROSPECT. EVERYONE WORKING THIS IS COUNTED AS A NETWORK MAILER. HELP WHERE NEEDED MOST IS A BETTER MOTIVATION. NETWORK MAILERS ARE COMMITTED TO FOLLOWING THESE INSTRUCTIONS.

POINTS

1). ON A PIECE OF PAPER, PRINT YOUR ADDRESS AND THIS NOTE, "ENCLOSED ARE 10 DOLLARS FOR YOU." MAIL IT AND 10 DOLLARS TO THE ADDRESS IN POSITION (1).

2). COPY THE ADDRESSES ON A PIECE OF PAPER; NOT ADDRESS (1).

3). COVER THE ADDRESSES WITH A PIECE OF PAPER ½ INCH WIDE.

4). REPRINT THE ADDRESSES; 2 IN 1, 3 IN 2. PRINT YOUR ADDRESS IN POSITION (3).

5). FOR A MASTER SHEET, COPY ON 24LB, BRIGHT, WHITE COPY PAPER.

6). MAIL 60 FLYERS IN #10 ENVELOPES, PER MONTH. THIS CAN RESULT IN $2,160,000.

7). REPEAT POINT 1) AS OFTEN AS YOU RECEIVE THIS IN YOUR MAIL.

8). SECURE A COMPUTER PRINTOUT OF THIS FLYER WHENEVER NECESSARY TO KEEP CLARITY OF THE PRINT. USE BOLD FONT 12 TYPE.

9). LET REPLIERS BECOME YOUR TOP PRIORITY MAILING LIST FOR REPEATS. THIS MARKET IS VERY HUGE. IT WOULD TAKE 500 YEARS TO MAIL TO 150,000,000 DIFFERENT ADDRESSES MAILING 300,000 YEARLY.

(1). _____

(2). _____

(3). _____

IT DON'T TAKE LONG FOR ADDRESS (3) TO BE IN POSITION (1). EVERY NETWORK MAILER HAVE THEIR TURN TO BE IN POSITION (1). AFTER (3) IS IN POSITION (1), A LOT OF 10 DOLLARS WILL FOLLOW FROM NETWORK MAILERS WORKING THIS FINANCIAL PROSPECT.

NETWORK MAILERS REPLYING TO NETWORK MAILERS INCREASES THE RATE OF REPLY AND THE FINANCIAL POTENTIAL. THE HUGE MARKET MAKES THIS FINANCIAL PROSPECT WORK. FOR A SOURCE OF REPLY PROSPECTS, WRITE TO THE FOLLOWING FOR A FREE COPY OF THEIR ADVERTISING MAGAZINE "SHORE TO SHORE': CHA SERVICES-P.O. BOX 1980 ROGUE RIVER, OR 97537 THE FINANCIAL POTENTIAL OF THIS BUSINESS IS WORTH THE WORKING OF IT.